Jeremy Hooker was born in the south of E.   . in 1941. He is a poet, critic, teacher and broadcaster. His ten previous collections of poetry include *A View from the Source: Selected Poems*, 1982, two collaborations with the sculptor Lee Grandjean (*Their Silence a Language*, 1993, and *Groundwork*, 1998), and *Our Lady of Europe*, published by Enitharmon in 1997. His critical books include monographs on David Jones and John Cowper Powys, *Poetry of Place* (1982), *The Presence of the Past: Essays in Modern British and American Poetry* (1987), and *Writers in a Landscape* (1996). Among his programmes for the radio are *Daring the Depths* and *A Map of David Jones*, and he has edited collections of writings by Alun Lewis and Frances Bellerby. His most recent books are *Imagining Wales: A View of Modern Welsh Writing in English* (University of Wales Press, 2001), a new selection of Richard Jefferies' later writings, *At Home on the Earth* (Green Books, 2001), and *Welsh Journal* (Seren, 2001). Jeremy Hooker has taught in universities in England, the Netherlands and the U.S.A., and is now Reader in English Literature and a professor at the University of Glamorgan.

Jeremy Hook (signature)

Jeremy Hooker

Adamah

For Ann
I enjoyed our reading!
Jerry

ENITHARMON PRESS

2002

First published in 2002
by the Enitharmon Press
26B Caversham Road
London NW5 2DU

www.enitharmon.co.uk

Distributed in the USA and Canada
by Dufour Editions Inc.
PO Box 7, Chester Springs
PA 19425, USA

ISBN 1 900564 52 1

British Library Cataloguing-in-Publication Data.
A catalogue record for this book is available
from the British Library.

Typeset in Bembo by Servis Filmsetting Ltd, Manchester
and printed in England by
The Cromwell Press

I made play in this world of dust, with the sons of Adam for my play-fellows.

The Book of Proverbs
Knox translation

In memory of my parents and my brother David

ACKNOWLEDGEMENTS

Some of these poems first appeared in *Fire, News for the Ear: A Homage to Roy Fisher* (Stride, 2000), *New Welsh Review, Notre Dame Review, Obsessed with Pipework, Planet, P.N. Review, Scintilla, 10th Muse, Thames: An Anthology of River Poems* (Enitharmon, 1999), *Writing in Education.*

'Keats in Winchester' is a new version of a section of 'A Winchester Mosaic', which appeared in my *Master of the Leaping Figures* (Enitharmon, 1987). The new version was first published in *Bright Star: Poems By and About John Keats* (Winchester City Council, 1995). An earlier version of 'Writers' Workshop' was written for, and appeared in, *Trying the Line: A Volume of Tribute to Gillian Clarke* (Gomer, 1997). A group of poems from 'Groundwork' was published in *Groundwork: Sculpture by Lee Grandjean and Poems by Jeremy Hooker* (Djanogly Art Gallery, University of Nottingham Arts Centre, 1998).

'Landscape of Childhood' was first broadcast on BBC Radio 3 in September 1991. I am grateful to Colin Edwards for detailed suggestions which helped me to revise the radio poem for publication.

CONTENTS

GROUNDWORK

for Lee Grandjean

Norfolk in April drought:
a cracked land.

Where do we begin?

Just here, say, at the point
in the fields where you see
the pinnacles of Salle church rise,
and Cawston, the naked stub
of the tower,
and the roofs of Moor Farm.

Just at this spot,
standing in a field
near the barn-studio
where oak trunks
are delivered, hitting
the brick floor with a 'dumb' sound
that pleases you.

Here, in a land of angels
carved from wood, and angels
sculpted in stone.

★

We begin at the end
of the story,
in millennial light.

Overhead on these clear April nights
the Comet's tail streams in the solar wind.

It is as if someone has opened a door
from which a light shines out
across the sky,
and into our minds

illuminating for an instant
images that have made us,
world on shattered world

and all around nebulae
are giving birth to stars.

★

Once more the visitor's book
confesses to a pilgrim
on the track of rumour, someone
who has come here seeking
the grave of Anne Boleyn.

SUNT LACRIMAE RERUM

The old song
would have us sing again
in throats that new song chokes.

★

*The dull mind rises to truth
through that which is material.*

Or when the mind is an image
of day without shadow,
no breeze to lift dust from the fields
or carry a seed to some moist place,
when you say to yourself
   I am this Thing,
this immovable block,
 and feel the weight of it
 and after a day of this,
 or a week, or a year,
    shake
yourself, and with a laugh,
shatter the thought, and,
brushing off the splinters,
     step out

★

How many times
the plough has gone through
the soil,
sped deep
in flinty loam

Christ alive
raised on
Adam's dust,
earth grassed
      seeded
          cropped

Word wrought in stone,
carved in wood,

don't you feel sometimes,
like an exhalation from dusty soil,
a sigh from all the acres,
all the depressions, and pits,
and pressing down of churches,
farm buildings,
don't you feel

the utter weariness of the dead?

★

What she said was:
God is nearer to us
than our own Soul:
for He is Ground
in whom our Soul standeth.

A green man pushed his head
out of the stonework, mouthing.
Angels and dragons flamed in the skies.

Shapes of belief
are still manifest
in empty niches,

makers
and image-breakers
show their hands.

★

In millennial light
wreckage
of an idea
littered on farmland
on concrete highrise
city dust and detritus

Millions becoming
one

Bones & blood
reassembling
a giant
blank-eyed

★

A day's work
is about to begin
under cross-beams
and rafters, in a space
once filled by horse-drawn carts
bringing hay or corn
from the fields.

Old iron things lie
in a corner – wheels,
parts of a ploughshare.
A rusted scythe hangs on the wall.

Oak trunks
partially shaped
stand on the floor.
Blades of light
flash down on them
like blazing swords.

★

What I want to argue
is that poetry and sculpture
are life sciences.

It is not that we express
some finished
or constructed self.

The point is to step out,
into the space between

★

I like the face of this
theoretical physicist
which appeared
            an abstraction
from an unknown and undefinable
totality
and has vanished
leaving us a theory –
a theatre –
in which we sense the whole

Shall we say, though,
a molecule of carbon dioxide
that crosses a cell boundary
                into a leaf
suddenly *comes alive*
and a molecule of oxygen
released to the atmosphere
suddenly *dies.*
Or shall we regard
life itself
as belonging
to a totality.

★

The man in the mirror is no one.
                He must get out,
stand in front of the block
                that is not himself,
wood that has its own ways,
that will take the shape he carves,
but retain its own nature.

                And in time
it will split, fissure,
shake the object he has made
which is not himself
and no longer a block of wood
but a thing that stands between

★

Or take words – Take words!
Words that run all ways,
                    spiderlines
which are at best a torn web,
or congealed in ice that freezes
heart and mind,
                    snowfield
pure of the faintest print,
in which, at the first step,
the dead will come dancing
and singing from their mounds.

★

SPEED THE PLOUGH
But no one now except
a solitary man driving a tractor
turns the soil
which lies folded in ridges,
dumb,
      bearing
mute trees,
church towers
foundering in the stillness
that has fallen on the land.

Stone angels stand on parapets
commanding gulfs of blue sky
and crumbling cloud.

Wooden angels stretch
in the hammerbeam roof,
each feather sensitively
carved alive,
but no one now to kindle
to imagined flight, swooping
like gulls in the wake of the plough

★

We do not deceive ourselves
that we are survivors
of an Age of Faith

or that searching for ground
is a metaphor
for meaning carried over

or that the blank page
is anything but blank

In millennial light
the ground is unimaginable

In what image can we make a shape?

Friendship, love, the self
gone out from the self

the man who has renounced power,
the woman who has assumed it,
            and let it go

The face in the mirror is no man's —
but someone has wandered out
and stands in front of the block,
someone who is,
you say, a wonderer

MOOR FARM: SUMMER 1996

August 5

Between garden and beck,
we walk in a field that still belongs to the moor.

With your painter's eye you see that masses
of rosebay willow herb – fireweed
of our childhood bomb-sites –
are white-violet among yellows, blues, rust-red.

Beyond the beck, straw bales
have been stacked in towers.
These surfaces are the deeps
of Norfolk,
field upon field upon field.

        I want to take all in,
forgetting the despair
that I know you too sometimes feel.

Late in the afternoon, a faint nimbus
of cloud floats high in the blue.
The red house, tiled roof and barn
black against the sky.

August 6

Downwind of where we walk, two hares,
with long, black-tipped ears,
sit listening.

Two military jets,
shaped like arrowheads,
fly in wide circles high overhead.

Together, after the attacks,
we can think of it: panic that springs
from a feeling of failure.

Losing direction in mid-speech,
between words; seeing only
a complex muddle, no way through.

A seed of madness falls from imagined air.

At dusk, I watch for the barn owl.

It flies towards me until its face
fills my vision, like a planet.

August 7

Tools on a bench: claw
gouge chisel mallet
club hammer bolster point

I say them over slowly
weighing them, testing edges.

Adze-marked rafters
and roof-beams high
over the work bench,
and in the space where carts
brought in corn and hay
in their seasons,
blocks, unhewn
or partially shaped
standing or lying
on the brick floor.

Not knowing
            is the way.
So you stand
in front of a block,
chisel in one hand,
mallet in the other

and all around you
is world as it was,
dust of an old image
pulverized.

Under your hand
the block, and you stand
not knowing,
blank to the voice that knows

and make a mark

City Walking (1)

for Roy Fisher

There is a looking that is
a kind of touch,
        a fingering
beyond the body's reach.

Near Paddington,
complexity of softly
growing cloud against
a builded concrete edge.

A giant's range
but we are small enough
among the press,

walking
       reaching out.

          ★

Between Edgware Road
and Liverpool Street,
in a cutting:
       buddleia,
a jungle of purple flowers
sprung from London brick.

          ★

A wind blows under Exchange House,
below steel arch and lit offices.

It blows from an older London,
out of undercuts and passageways,
across abraded facades
and worn York paving,
through railway bridges.

It plays on
work-in-progress
on a steel skeleton,
cranes reaching high,
and, glistering,
the fuselage of a jet.

★

This place, you tell me,
is your idea of world
as it will be after you have gone.

But wind still blows round
the high buildings
of black glass and steel.

And here, tangled from his fall,
is a sculpture of one more hero
who tried to fly to heaven.

★

The brown Thames
laps against timbers.

A fragment of Roman wharf
is bound against a pillar,
ancient water-worn wood
against carved stone.

Inside St Magnus Martyr,
splendour
of Ionian white and gold.

I listen for the music
that the poet heard.
From memory, I piece
the fragments of a song.

★

Passing where the boat went down,
it was not your dream you told me,
or mine, but I had to follow,
                    down.

Man out of air, choking.

How slowly death comes,
though it was minutes since he stood,
glass in hand,
charming and enchanted.

A sleeper on a bench
beside the river, struts
digging in his side,
turns restlessly
as the half-dead man
who dreamt that he was drowning
pops up, seal-headed, the city
with its millions of feelers
ready once more to take him in.

                    ★

For indeed it is everywhere death
that uncovers its plague-pits
and ashes and unclaimed corpses.

Death and the desire
that clasps us in the press
or shoots us full of glances
or holds us water-mouthed
in front of images that consume.

Ebb tide reveals where London has crumbled.

Things once animate with use
are sheer matter, glutinous, unshaping:
brick, plastic, iron, rope, wire;
granite sets of a causeway,
ground down, washing away.

London on London
sunk in Thames mud.
                    Yet each set
is also a way for the vagrant mind.

★

Red, purple, lilac,
hand-crafted, laid:

the beauty of brick,
brittle,
          crazed.

Haunted.

★

A man in the rush,
sent sprawling by another,
lands at my feet
on grey, spittled platform,
lurches up and is gone.
And in the instant, before
I can reach out a hand,
we are all of us one
sea-bed of identical skulls
over which grey silt
settles and congeals.

★

Walking between the New Globe
and the river, I think of the old man
and the son who leads him,
on the Dover Road,
bringing him to the edge
of a high cliff, from which he jumps.

What an imagined fall!

Walking in the city that is continually
being made and unmade,
I think of the cliff
which Edgar built of words,
and his father's leap,
down,

      down . . .

★

To see
      by way of words.

Stile and gate,
horse way and foot path.

Do you hear the sea?

Here's the place.

★

The poet's river glides by
or oozes stickily under the wall.

It is also what exists
in the eyes of a cormorant
perching on a floating platform
above Westminster Bridge.

★

The old man
is full of stories.

In this place,
Julius Caesar's men
waded across the river,
and Saxons built a church
on what was then an island
of hard gravel, washed
by the river and surrounded
by miles of marsh.

The same from whose soil
Catherine Boucher's family
made their market garden –

Catherine, who, in this church,
married William Blake.

And here (our guide shows us
the vestry window) Turner
sat to paint clouds
and sunsets over the water –

where we can see tower blocks,
luxury flats, a marina,
a power station
that drives the Underground.

The old man too was married here,
twice; and his daughter
was christened, and wed . . .

As he talks, the empty church
fills silently with shadows.

It is a relief, then,
to walk on the shore
under the churchyard wall,
and look at houseboats, geese
in the water, and watch a tug
powering upriver, drawing
a barge with containers of waste.

At Battersea Bridge,
a heron flies over, mirrored
in a building of steel and black glass.

★

All in the head
so to speak,
the sacred head –
                other world
by which this world lives.

Offerings to the river-god,
father of many parts,
many changes:

a horned helmet,
a bronze shield.

Centuries will flow over them,
silt accumulate,
city on city
stand
        changing shape.

★

Excavations
for power lines,
office blocks.

A head of Mithras,
traces of temple walls,
bull and bear bones,
human bones.

Voices out of air,
imagined air,
becoming vessels,
houses, journeys
underground.

★

The city is also lives we do not lead.

In the Kyoto Garden,
a beautiful woman with red hair
walks elegantly, alone,

and in the time it takes her
to pause on the stone bridge
under the cascade,

we have become lovers, although
she will never know who I am
or how much damage we have caused.

★

Upstairs, in the front seat
of a bus, streets and houses
swinging round us, acacia branches
brushing the glass,
I see you: a boy
kicking a stone, playing
on bomb sites, fingering
a stone in your pocket:
looking, feeling the edge
of a concrete building
against softly growing cloud.

★

You tell me not to look back
until we are high
on Primrose Hill, turning
to see a scattering
of small lights, black
middle distance, and behind,
in a wide arc, towering blocks,
the shell of St Paul's,
far at the back
Canary Wharf,
a luminous triangle
in the sky.

A greeny grey phosphorescence
in lit windows conceals
unimaginable lives.
Over all, one sound –
a constant hum –
absorbs our words.

Sharp and bright
above petrol dusk
the evening star.

SEVEN SONGS

City Walking (2)

for Sarah Hemming and Julian May

Today I imagine her walking,
seven months pregnant, resting
from the effort of working with her husband,
in their terraced house in Old Woolwich Road,
preparing a room for the baby.

Down narrow, brick lanes she wanders,
past iron bollards, like cannons stood on end,
behind her the Royal Observatory on the hill,
across the river, on the Isle of Dogs,
Canary Wharf gleaming, dominating the sky.
And here are gantries, industrial chimneys,
almshouses, immaculate in the shadow
of a power station with dirty white, peeling walls.

Through a gate at Highbridge Drawlock,
down a slipway, onto a shore of shingle
and sand, where she stoops, fingering
shards of pottery and brick,
glass jewels, among the stones.

    Low waves flop over,
swirl round a rowing boat swinging on a rope.
Sunlight glitters in millions of eyes.

    It is peaceful here, the city
is a distant rumble; traffic,
railway, power station, refinery,
corn mill, voices – all one sound.

I let my mind move with hers over the water,
past seaweedy, green walls and piles,
converted wharves, leisure complexes,
docks, offices to let, stone church spires,
past woodwork, ironwork, ladders
descending into the water.

               Today she is in love
with the city and the river,
joining and dividing, flowing through.
Silently she recites the names of bridges:
Tower Bridge London Bridge Southwark
Blackfriars Waterloo,
                    her mind drifting
until she sees a heron on the deck of a rusting barge
and the sight fixes her.

Sunlight in millions of eyes
glittering on the surface, through which she sees
the water's body, and feels
the channelled weight, the wild
and voiceless mother tongue.

I would follow if I could, out of the sight
of fixed and finished things, power
and after-images of power;
out of the city fractured
and constructed – the city
that is not one, but shaped to millions of needs.

For a moment only I think she enters
the place where no one can dwell,
the dark tide that generates,
pushing into gaps and inlets, carrying
driftwood, silt,

and emerges, rested, strolling home.

BEFORE THE DAY SET HARD

In sleep, I cried –

I was a story that was being told,
a fugitive that fled with bleeding legs
and felt a hot breath on my neck
and on my back the thwack of staves.

I ran and ran but could not move.
My body was a beaten bush,
in which I hid, a tiny bird.

And woke. Or seemed to wake,
sleep's waters parting as I felt for ground.

And now I walked in fields above the sea,
a place of furze and granite tombs,
each Cyclops-cave an eye of dark.

And there I saw the Sun in Majesty,
that melted as I watched,
a molten rain that fell in gold drops on the sea,
and cloud that mushroomed into space,
and turbulence of cloud,
a chalice spilling poisons on the earth.

Where I looked west,
the salt fields of the deep
were Lyonesse, and palaces
of tangled wrack, and leaping rocks
were dolphins turned to stone,
or submerged effigies of ancient knights.
And overall a wounded tanker
wallowed, bleeding oil.

I walked upon the cliffs
and heard a small bird sing,
a jingle and a trill that rose and fell,
a strident churr.

Don't ask or seek to know, a voice said then.
The story being told is what you are.

I trod the waters of a dream,
and reached for ground, and heard
the strange voice say:
**You are a woman at the door of time.
Imagine, then, anew**.

Then in a dark-mouthed tomb,
a Cyclops-eye, I saw an eye,
a tiny, bright and living thing.
I saw a cocked-tail flit,
and sensed, so near, a clutch
of breast-warm eggs that nestled
in a globe of moss and down.

So near, before the day set hard –
         but must it set?

Or shall I tell the story as I choose,
and walk on cliffs above the main,
and see the sparks of furze, and feel with her,
the hunted bird that dwells in caves,
the bird who makes her nest inside the tomb?

CYANE

Finally a body that is water's own.

So at times words seem to come to me,
as though I could speak,
or as I remember speaking in another life.

I pool to a glassy stillness.
I move slowly, mirroring
shapes & colours of leaves;
housefronts, walls; a face;
the world entranced
gazing at the world.

Or quick, a stream
of silver – only
what I know is imageless,
except once, in another life . . .

My moods are stagnant,
turbulent. I circle circle circle,
or stand motionless, or pour out,
falling, scattering,
coming together with the smoothness
of a dolphin's back, an icy glide.

What was I before I was finally this?
Sometimes I dream that on my surface
I form a human face,
and look out at another,
red and glistening, a man's,
and arms, in which he grasps a woman,
binds her to him, drags her down.

And it shakes then: earth quakes,
and springs apart – they are gone.

And I shake, the being that I was –
skin blood bones
unbinding, flying into drops,
flowing with a constant tremor,
plunging down, shattering,
shaking out long and smooth,
always broken, always whole.

And over I go and over,
and under, and round and round.

But what is that but a dream
that I was human once,
who am pure spirit,
not bodied, not bodiless,
but water in water, quick
with a life beyond all words.

Silence, then; or a voice
that is the sound of water running,
in which, if they listen,
any one may hear a tale
of terror at the roots of things:

a tale that I tremble to tell,
half remembering, or inventing,
but as if, once, it were my own.

LAND'S END

'. . . in the sea nothing lives to itself.'
                    Rachel Carson

She has saved her body from the sea
once more, but feels engirdled still,
tangled with wrack,
bound with straps of kelp
whose loose ends slap her legs
as once again she clambers up the shore
and feels beneath her feet
the final grains of sand,
the hidden matrices.

So consciousness returns.

But as her head emerged from webs of foam,
sleek in the swell,
                    what had she seen?
Rock stacks, sheer falls,
chance balancings of rock on rock;
rock flattened, rounded,
scooped out, split,
                    a spectacle
of camelbacked and giant shapes,
ribbed matter historied and named,
headland pharos and the chambered tombs . . .
Then – closer – quartz
and crystal sparkle, mica shine,
the sun a blade laid on the sea.
And, in a stroke of dark,
the meltdown world,
Plutonic depths,
the serpent fire, long cooling

that no mind can see,
the blank face of the rock.

And what she sees is blank.
Earth an island made of cloud,
no ground, but everywhere –
ghost sun in mist –
a bone mask showing through.

But what is this?
Half fish, half woman, carved in wood,
a man's embodied knowledge
in the cutting touch,
a feel of salty flesh –
which she stands looking at,
and hears windrush of breaking waves
and feels again the labour
of the tide,
and then the long pull out
beyond land's end,
as she takes leave,
at liberty to ride the deep,
and once more save her body from the sea.

BETWEEN WORLDS

Earthbound, she thinks; all power
gone into the ground – sheepmen
and their wives, flocks of sheep
on whose backs the building was raised . . .

And if any soul could come back now
and find me in their place?

Outside, she sees a wild man
with a club held across his chest.
And here are angels – they are scaly,
and might be mermaids, but
the scales are armour – they are warriors,
their wingtips pointed, like fern.
Old gods and the young god
and his cohort, she thinks –
                    and one visitor
with her hand on the latch.

Inside, tall pew ends catching
her sight are, momentarily,
a large congregation.
Space releases her spirit,
a familiar musty smell brings it down.

If any soul could return, moving
invisibly between worlds,
and meet her
where she stands looking down,
not questioning, but a question
to herself . . . What am I?
What do I want in this place?

But there is no one here,
and if there were, she thinks,
how desolate the soul finding her
would be; how dank with the tears of things
the damp-spotted stone,
the emptiness.

No one. Then, for an instant,
she feels fury frozen
into wood and stone; fury
of image-breakers – in niches,
violently emptied,
statues flung down,
carvings, faces smashed,
brasses levered out, leaving
human shapes set in the floor.
Through plain glass she can see
wind streaming through grass growing over graves.

And now she is walking away into the wind
that drives clouds over.
                    And to her eyes
it is as though the wind
were shaping all she sees –
curves of the land
and dark, wooded hollows,
whirlpools among corn,
stone angels on the roof
                    flying.

                    And it is as though
the tower were an island
in a blue gulf, and she,
eyes and ears filled by the wind,
were a leaf blown from a twig
and whirled away.

GROUNDLESS SHE WALKS

Her footstep strikes
the dusty track.
        Heat-haze
on ripening wheat creates
a shimmer in which the gorged pigeon
flaps away losing shape.
In dark places, in their own spheres,
minute creatures webbed in moisture
vibrate at her burdened tread.
And she feels down through cracked earth,
knowing something about them, sensing
the rhythms by which they live.
And what, she thinks, are their constellations,
what gods burn in their heavens?
Do they too know a Cassiopeia who holds up her arms?
Are they companioned, or unsupported
except by physical law,
sheer materiality, lumpen as flints
which will indifferently turn my ankle
or break a plough?
        Instability
was the mark of the day when she woke.
She has been at the edge
since first light crazed mirror and window glass,
froze the lightning of the garden tree
against the toppling tidal wave of earth.
She is a woman carrying a child who flinches
at the momentary thought she is a man
who dreams herself to be a woman,
and who now is walking beside a harvest field,
kicking up the dust,
                alone, afraid.

43

What is possible? she insists, feeling
again the movement under her heart.
                    Who was it said
'the march of time'?
Months weeks days hours minutes seconds
hard boots striking sparks from flint
regiments tramping from the cave-mouth
                    down the years.
And must it be so, faces
with the same blind look ever
appearing, disappearing – one likeness
dominant as Jupiter in the night-sky?

An obstruction in the flow: blackness
shot through with flashes of light,
scintillations,
her mind itself the sky
in which a woman lifts up her hands
over heavy-headed wheat,
the whole sea of the field whispering.

But she may not dissolve;
she must absorb turbulence;
the desire within to be other
is the pressure she must bear.

But must the story repeat itself,
the flame be kindled to burn as one
with the whole fire that consumes and dies?
Let me take a seed of thought
and find for it a cryptic niche,
some damp place under soil or under bark,
a home of bacteria, of creatures
that live in water, and grow there
a being that moves to another rhythm . . .

But now her mind is an ice-berg
in a polar sea, mountainous dark
moving under her, bearing her along.

And instantly the image fractures,
and dissolves.

What, then, is possible? she cries
silently, as groundless her footstep
strikes the dusty track.

The child I carry
will crawl into the world.
What ground will he stand on?
What humus, or piece of debris
hurtling from the supernova,
the giant star that once was man?

THE SEVENTH SONG

'Life is what we never see.'
Michel Henry

**The seventh song
is groundlessness.**

Born out of language
it came, as though a poem
were a bloody birth,
its mother more than words.

Fingering a stick,
rounding the hand to a hold, it came.
Stick that digs in a ditch.
You know who it is that digs, making a hole.

But what is this? Noise of traffic
out there. In here
you go right down, you reach
into the smell of the hole, soil
tickle-whiskering your face.
In here you go right down to a place
that is not the world.

Other sounds, too, make
the seventh song.
Crump
of bombs, mosquito whine
that belongs with the roughness
of blankets, under ground,
recoil of the guns
that rock your cradle,
and the Welsh gunner's tenor voice,
which you hear only
because you were told about it,
singing in the field.

What you loved most was touch:
the feel of earth: dark crumbs
on which the spirit feeds.
                    In that sense
the way leads back, into chalk,
into earth that is humped, mounded,
into stone dwellings where they sit
in their birthday skeletons,
with their hand-axes
and ornaments made of animal teeth.

Bullrush gravel-pit waters
rise in the mind. Without these,
without the first Moses-basket,
there would be no seventh song.
And there is that, that only,
a boy-girl feeling no one can ever see.

There is what the flow is made of:
scribbles on a wall,
a note left on a pillow,
indecipherable,
written to say:
I have gone to see the world.

And there you are: on the sea-wall,
having crapped and wiped your backside
with a handful of grass,
and now running up and down
waving a piece of seaweed.

                Without this,
there would be no seventh song.

What it sings is a way,
a growing that is a growing round.
As seasons are in wood,
present tissue –
                    that day
in wartime, babies in a pram,
cousins, a boy and a girl; the sun
that enters under the coverlet,
revealing nothing but itself,
pavement over which the wheels bump –
nothing that is any more
than what it is felt to be.

Or footsteps where shingle moves,
time in time that can be seen,
almost,
            sift of tiny pebbles,
shells, infant green carapaces,
evacuated of life.
But it cannot be seen in these,
nor in water that eats the substance
out of sea-walls, water
that moves, laps, flows.

However fluent, it cannot be seen
in the song, nor in this or that,
the hole or the digging stick,
the place down under,
in this world,
which you would learn one day
to call the Antipodes.

**The seventh song
is groundlessness.**

But it is here, look,
in your hands,
which are perfectly empty.

FROM DEBRIS: A CYCLE OF POEMS

FROM DEBRIS

From debris
of collapsing stars,
from gas and dust,
where nothing is wasted,
a stream of images.

GROUND-IVY

Hobnailed
imprinting the soil,
Adamah stops,
bound to the spot,
wondering at the tiny
smoke-blue flower
that bears his mother's name.

NIGHT PIECE

Cut of farm roofs, black
against sunset,

owl hoot sounding
the depth of woods:

the present is a blade
you could try with your thumb.

It is a haunting thought
that there are no ghosts,

only this black and shining edge.

Owl Country

Where the beck trails
alders and dark,
feather-headed reeds,
at the foot of a post,
a pellet:
compacted fur,
yellow teeth
with which a vole
would gnaw
      no more.

Feathered deaths

On the concrete floor,
three heaps of feathers,
pied wagtails
that found their way in.

The view through the window
seems endless, a pathway
through sky over the planet,
the flowing cloud.

LARK SONG

Springing
from clod and flint

rising
invisible

or a black dot
quivering

raining over
and all around

song shower
in April air.

LUCKY STRIKE

Returning from a raid,
just missed the tower
where, over the West Door,
the Wild Man with oak leaves
wound round his body
faces the Dragon
            wreathed in vines.

Crash landed at Church Farm,
ploughing itself in,
churning up the loam.
Two crew dead.
            The Flight Engineer
periodically revisits
the old country, resuming
his portion of the pasture.

ANGELS AT SALLE

I feel for them:
        spirits
bodied in stone, motionless
winged beings the wind abrades,

soldiers standing at their post
on a long-abandoned field.

PALIMPSEST

Hand-painted,
the stories of death
and resurrection;
in the margin,
matters of business,
manorial accounts:
fodder, grain, sheep.
Requiem eternam . . .
et lux perpetua.
Here, too, in the light
of workaday transactions
the poetry of meaning.

MAGNOLIA

Flowers opening,
foxglove-red at base,
creamy shell-like petals

scatter your images on the ground
where the tree springs,
flowers erect,

where it moves in you
and the only word
you feel in your mouth
is **tongue.**

FOR QUICKNESS

Observation (looking at the magnolia) can become an idol.

Why should seeing be painful, unless one is possessive, wanting to
see all?

It is feeling with, feeling into, that respects the other.

Distance makes this possible. There is no other way of coming close.

PASTORAL

A field gate,
five bars of weathered oak,
goose grass cleaving to them,

a gate stuck open
permanently,
rusted chain hanging.

Once the way
from the fields to the horse pond
in its semi-circle of ash-trees;
from the pond
to woods solid with shadow,
through woods to the church,
stone wildmen and dragons,
to labourers' homes.

You may say it opens on
a world that is dead.
I would reply that,
like the goose grass,
this is where I like to be.

CROPS

Early one August morning
he inspected his crops.

In a cornfield
due to be harvested,
a rectangular shape
had formed in the dew
and with it, across his land
a legion of ghosts.

Later,
sun dried the grain
leaving only a crop
to be gathered in.

SCULPTOR'S WORKSHOP

We stand at the end of a long time
looking back through a telescope.

Galaxy collides
with galaxy,
a shock wave speeds out.

Inside the spiral arms
old stars are dying.

Bright in the blue ring,
from dust and gas,
stars are being born.

NOT NEWTON

The old bramley
bowed down
under the weight
of big apples

a red admiral
feeding on
a windfall

a green woodpecker
flying away
laughing

nothing
but
energy.

HARE

Fear of us makes
the heart jump,
the body leap, the long legs
run uphill, and stand —

Absolute hare,
long ears laid back,
long skull, our image
a gleam in dark eyes.

Whether birds feel joy in their flight

Whether one's lifework might be something no one wants

Whether one will end up living in a cardboard box

Whether love is an element like air or fire

Such are the questions on their purple tongues.

QUICK DANCERS

Brief chaotic spirals
formed of the dust of the ground,

dancers born of wind
and loose soil

which rise, flinging
themselves into the air,

almost natural phenomena
in which you believe,

picturing rhythm
and image: breathing life

into quick dancing figures
formed of the dust of the ground.

HOGWEED

Skeletal
on a hedgebank
against darkening sky

you imagine it
a wizard's wand
to conjure up the wind and snow

a telescope
to focus on
the Christmas star

a pipe
in fingers
stiff as ice
to play the New Year in.

READING WALLS

A late summer evening
darkens, light rain begins
to fall, swallows wheel
over us where we peer
at walls webbed with age
and feel with our fingers
signatures, initials,
names hand-cut in brick,
rough lines of those
who made the track
through the fields, dug clay
from the pit, wielded
the rusted scythe
that hangs on the barn wall
under the swallows' nests.

EARTHLING

How many space craft
have left for far destinations,

planetary, heavenly,
ideas carrying their cargoes

of visionary beings
who will not return.

Far-seeing, or new-born dead
in your shrouds,

I am your fellow,
strange as you are,

but let me stay, smelling
earth and pond water at dusk.

STANDING UPRIGHT

Two-legged
walking
stretching
like a tree
but not rooted
like fence post
telegraph pole
but not fixed
something
with an inside
made of darkness
speaking hand
dumb mouth
closing
        opening

Autumn

Spiderlines appear
in the garden overnight.

She might have spun them
herself, so carefully

she moves, taking
the whole new garden in.

Leap

Day is blown through
by a wind that scours,
a wind that reveals.

Cloud is driven over,
sky clears,
and in the instant
imagination cuts
a shape of belief.

LANDSCAPE OF CHILDHOOD

A poem for radio

First broadcast on BBC Radio 3, 13 September 1991

Cast

Mother:	Sonia Woolley
Father:	Christopher Robbie
Peter:	Jeremy Hooker
David:	Tom Durham

Producer: Julian May

INTRODUCTION

In writing this poem for radio, I called to mind the places of my childhood: the shingly shore at Warsash, the chalk Downs, which I first glimpsed as something dazzling, strange and wonderful, New Forest heaths and woods, the brook, the great rivers of the south, Southampton after the blitz. First, the places I recalled presented themselves to me as things: flint-stones, the earth of a ditch, mammoth bones, gravelly soil in a strawberry field, sea shells and ocean liners, shrapnel, Spitfires and Heinkels. It was only gradually that I realized how much the shape of the landscape in my mind owed to words spoken by other people.

I started to tell a story, which concerns my father who was a painter, and my mother who instilled a love of poetry in me when I was very young. How could I distinguish my first impressions of the landscape from his paintings? The words of the poems, too, became part of the places. I developed a theme around my eldest brother's fascination with aeroplanes and flight, and my contrasting attraction to earth and water, to the darkness that roots grow down into, and to quick, reflecting, fluid surfaces. The story I told was fiction, but based on fact. But as I wrote I realized that many of the facts, too, were contained in stories, the stories which my parents told me, often about their childhoods, and their parents and *their* childhoods. So, what is past? What is present? The places existed in fact, formed by geology, made by history, but for me they were also voices of family and ancestral experience. The landscape of childhood, which was the foundation of my life, consisted of other lives, and was shaped for me by loved voices. In writing the poem, that was the truth I saw and heard.

PETER: Wartime in southern England.
It is then and now and long ago.
I will paint you a picture at the edge of darkness,
construct for you places that are made of sound.
Do not imagine that what you hear is true.
It is not words alone that make a poem.

This is where I begin.
I am the boy who picks a laurel leaf,
bends it, pushing the stalk through veined flesh.
Now I launch my boat on the brook,
watch it bump on pebbles, snag on a twig,
twist free and glide swiftly away,
riding the current round the bend and out of sight.

Light and shadow flicker.
I am a keel slicing through mud.
I begin here, at the edge of darkness.
The brook gurgles in its bed.
It is not words alone, or things,
but human voices that shape the world.

FATHER: What is that in the air?
What hurtles down?
Friend or foe, friend or foe?

MOTHER: *A fair little girl sat under a tree*
Sewing as long as her eyes could see,
Then smoothing her work and folding it tight
She said 'Dear work, goodnight, goodnight'.

PETER: A high, blue day in late summer.
Gulls pick between pill-box and wire.
Barrage balloons with elephant ears
tug at their moorings, puff out their cheeks.
Where the estuary crawls seaward
longships and galleys lie under.

Ships of the line that sailed from
this shore — once forest oaks, barnacle-
crusted — lie fathoms deep among cannons
sunken in primeval woods. Above,
warplanes approach the coast.

FATHER: Look at the river. See how it runs
with light and shadow. A Summer Day
on the Avon. The Wylye in Autumn.
A Quiet Day on the Boldre River.
Tree trunks tremble and flicker
with reflected water-light.
Sky and river flow together
with sedge and grass and trees.
You must have your eye on the subject
for the love of it. That is seeing.
That is what being an artist means.

PETER: What was the river before he painted it?
That flowing stillness of blue
and green and feather-white.
What was the shore?
That green on yellow of weedy shingle,
West Wight and the Needles like galleons
carved out of chalk.

MOTHER: The Island was always there, even when
it wasn't — if you see what I mean. Hidden
in mist, it was always there for us
when we were children. Whenever we looked
out, the Island was there. Always.
Never the same.

> *Time, like an ever-rolling stream,*
> *Bears all its sons away;*
> *They flie forgotten, as a dream*
> *Dies at the opening day.*

66

PETER: In my sleep I hear the sounds of it,
           swish of wave on shingle,
           tinkle of gravel, grind and roar,
           juddering knock on breakwater,
           and always in it and over it all
           the ghost of grey waters,
           bright angel of scavengers,
                       the black-headed gull.

FATHER: I started off at Ringwood
           and went away down the valley –
           painted the bridge at Ibsley.
           I saw light coming through the trees,
           darkest part under the arch. I painted
           elms too. Destroyed them. Didn't care
           for the subject finally. You must love
           what you see.

PETER: Once upon a time
           my brother carried me out at night
           and pointed at the sky. High up,
           among the stars, a white star moved,
           grew and glowed brighter,
           then fell apart – a brief, bright shower
           flamed and faded.
           What am I? What is this place?
           Gulls cry. A siren wails.
           I hear voices telling stories.
           I pick a laurel leaf and make a boat
           and launch it on the brook.
           I am a keel slicing through mud,
           feeling a blind way down. I too
           may have a story to tell: together,
           our voices shaping the world.

FATHER: What is the sea disgorging?
          What is that lying in the windrow
          with crabshells and cockles?

MOTHER: *She saw her brother Peterkin*
                  Roll something large and round
              Which he beside the rivulet
                  In playing there had found;
              He came to ask what he had found
              That was so large and smooth and round.

              Old Kaspar took it from the boy
                  Who stood expectant by;
              And then the old man shook his head,
                  And with a natural sigh
              'Tis some poor fellow's skull,' said he,
              'Who fell in the great victory'.

DAVID: A pack of Heinkels crosses the coast.
          I crouch in a culvert. Shrapnel
          whines overhead, spits in the brook.
          Spitfires flash among vapour trails in the sun.
          The ground is slipping away beneath me.

              You are my sunshine, my only sunshine.
              You make me happy when skies are grey.
              You'll never know, dear, how much I love you.
              Please don't take my sunshine away.

          Down below, small fields:
          the back-breaking, sweating earth.
          Down there, all the drag –
          sea slopping on breakwaters,
          trees' nervous roots fingering
          down, gripping the soil.
          But here in the sky the cords fly loose.

Blue and green and silver
the world spins around me.
    And out of the sun
springs the swastika'd hunter.
I crouch in the culvert.
Shrapnel bites the path by
the brook, blasts dust from clods
of earth in Pegrim's field.

MOTHER: I was taken outdoors one night to see
    a thing in the sky that looked
    to me like a silver fish –
    they told me it was a zeppelin –
    held in lights as it glided
    over the downs near Winchester.
    That was the year my mother died –
    winter, 1917; my father broke ice
    from the windowsill of her room
    and touched it to her lips, but
    it was no good, the doctor shook
    his head, it would be useless to call again.
    She died; the baby was born dead,
    the nurse gave it to me to hold,
    like a doll . . . people didn't always
    know better then . . .

> *You are my sunshine, my only sunshine,*
> *You make me happy when skies are grey.*
> *You'll never know, dear, how much I love you.*
> *Please don't take my sunshine away.*

DAVID: Up and up,
    through cloud and over it,
    over the white cloudscapes, I roll
    in blue sky and glimpse the earth
    through drifts and chasms, the Island shrinks

to a mound, dromes like backyards on
the heaths . . .
Behind and below me, slipping away,
the cumulus of the downs.
And I am free of it all, shining
among vapour trails; like a child
dreaming, arms outstretched,
soaring and diving.

FATHER: I set up my easel on the shingle.
At Warsash. At Keyhaven.
    But it wasn't the sea
I loved finally.
Too turbulent. I love peace.
A Quiet Day on the Boldre River.
Look at the water. See how it flows
with light and shadow –
blue and green and feather-white,
the darkest dark under the bridge.
I painted what I saw – fearlessly.

PETER: Where mammoth bones were dredged
from dockland, they loom at me,
the great liners:
Mauretania, Berengaria, Titanic.
And sometimes I swim in the boiling
dark green iceberg sea and go down, down,
as if the water were skyscraper
piled on skyscraper where I fall
slowly till on the Atlantic floor
I touch with blind fingers the doomed
steel sides and sense above me
the fallen tower of the funnel . . .
Who screamed? I wake shuddering,
with aching arms and legs, hearing

in dockland streets, awash
with bitter cold, the first gull's
                    laughing cry.

DAVID: A lone Lysander from Lee-on-Solent
            droned along the coast before the war.
            I can't describe what I felt.
            Tiger moths falling out of the sky,
            falling and falling, silent as leaves,
            then the engine firing, the plane
            easing out level, beginning to climb,
            and once – an arm waving,
            a helmeted head looking down at me.

PETER: Overnight, in the city centre,
            shops and houses vanish.
            The earth lies open. There are pits
            of gravel and clay, with a bit
            of someone's bedroom wall, strips
            of wallpaper hanging.
            The fuselage of a plane on the shore.
            Shrapnel on the garden path,
            a dud incendiary nose down
            among potato haulms.
            People gather with prams carrying
            babies and belongings
            under Forest trees;
            like gypsies, but out of place.

            I dig in a ditch beside the lane
            where tanks rumble through.
                    Strange men
            with tired, friendly faces
            wave from turrets, throw
            packets of gum. I poke
            the dark soil and it crumbles.

MOTHER: I was rooted to the ground.
           I could not move from the garden,
           but stood transfixed,
           holding the child in my arms.
           And down it came. Down. Screaming.
           I closed my eyes. Dead
           and the child dead with me.
           Then the earth shook. Silence.
           Your father ran out into the field,
           Pegrim's field, where, summer after
           summer before the war, we picked
           strawberries.
           Three generations of women, all
           with handkerchiefs tied over our heads
           to protect us from the sun.
           The pilot was still strapped in
           when your father reached him.
           He died in his arms.

PETER: One day, blinding white, the chalk rises.
           Barrows echo the downs against the sky.
           Cloud rolls on cloud.
           It is like first snow, stretching
           to the curve of the world.
           But under, the dark is fathomless.
           Sponges, fish delicate as feathers,
           hang locked in black cold.
           What fire will melt this frozen sea?
           At night the burning towns
           are campfires along the coast.
           Clouds and the waves roll on,
           phosphorescent, quick with new light.
           I find a domed fossil on the shore,
           a shepherd's crown.
           It is a seed from which the world

72

might grow anew one day,
rising up with dazzling sides.

MOTHER: When he was a boy my father earned
threepence from a farmer for scaring
rooks off his corn, and lost the coin
in the field, and went back
and found it . . .
He was born at a place called Toyd
on the Wiltshire border.
All his family were labourers.
I can't describe it, but somehow
I feel something stir in my blood
when I see the downs.
He was part of them, I am part of him.
He said he wouldn't have a stone
put up to mark his grave. If people
cared to remember him, they would.

PETER: What I love about flints is their shape:
a Stone Age palm in the curve, a pick
carved from a reindeer antler.
There are urns under the heath
that heather and gorse root in –
cracked eggs of some giant, primeval reptile.
My hands caress them in the dark.

> *But one morning very early*
> *Before the sun was up,*
> *I rose and found the shining dew*
> *On every buttercup.*
>
> *But my lazy little shadow*
> *Like an arrant sleepy head*
> *He had stayed at home behind me*
> *And was fast asleep in bed.*

FATHER: When I was a boy I went to bed
          with a candle and lay awake listening
          to foxes barking. At dawn I heard
          the cock crow and birds singing.
          I thought it would last for ever.
          When I was six years old my parents
          sent me across the fields with a wreath
          to a house where a coachman had died.
          They wouldn't go near him when
          he was alive; he swore at everyone.
          When he was dead they sent me.
          Walking home alongside the hedge
          I suddenly looked up – a big,
          red-orange ball hung in the sky.
          What was it? Later I knew,
          I had seen the sun for the first time.

MOTHER: What I loved best were the cart-horses.
          When I woke up I could hear them
          through the wall, stamping
          and shaking their heads.
          My sisters and I used to play
          around and even under them.
          They wouldn't hurt us or anyone
          with their big feathered hooves.
          But my father couldn't save them.
          they had to go – every one
          sent to the front
          to draw supplies and guns.

PETER: Sometimes I think I see the old man
          with his pony and trap, on the gravel track
          where the dual carriageway crosses the flyover –
          where the floating-bridge used to be.
          It is then and now and long ago.
          A siren wails. Gulls cry.

I hear voices telling stories.
This is where I begin. I seem to have known
the place always. Never the same.
It is not words alone, or things,
that make the poem. There is a sense
before words in which the poem begins.
Together our voices shape the world.

MOTHER: *A number of rooks flew over her head*
            Crying caw, caw on their way to bed.
            She said as she watched their curious flight,
            'Little black things, goodnight, goodnight'.

DEDICATIONS

WALKING TO SLEEP

A poem for my mother

Hours before you died,
I read you once more the poem
you first read to me
in which the merman mourns
for his human wife
who has left the sea
and will not come away,
down, down, who will not come away.

Then you, whose life
had been to care and comfort,
were walking to sleep –
                    walking,
counting the stones the shells
dog whelk cuttle-bone
shepherd's crown
fairy loaves anything
of interest on the shore
in sight of the Island
in sound of the sea.

Walking, walking down
where, hours before,
you heard a voice that said
'Start again, Start again'.

★

This is the shore
on which you loved to walk
in childhood, as a woman
with a family, and in age.

Walking
in love and in sorrow,
not looking away, but finding
in yourself the place
where you were most alone.

Walking, and always finding
something of interest –
driftwood, pulse of sunlight
in water, gull floating
on the swell.

What I think of now
is that place,
and of you watching, listening,
as I cast your ashes on the sea.

★

Your father was the same,
wanting no stone to mark his life.

Was it humility, or pride?
I only know he lived in you,
as you live in me.

Here are countless stones
and on all and every one
the print of memory . . .

What can I say that is not untrue?

You gave me my love of poetry,
and with it, the knowledge
that words are a shore
on which one must walk to the end,
and look far out, hoping
to glimpse the thing, the being
that one loves, and must let be.

★

Ash and specks of bone,
which a breeze blows back,
making a grey smear
on dry shingle,
which the next wave covers.

Yes, the tide is coming in,
the next wave leaps farther
up the shore, sluices
the shingle as it slides.

Beyond the swash,
the tinkling, shifting stones,
a gull dives down
out of the bright, late sun
and settles on the sea – one gull that seems
to have the whole bay to float on.

★

The martins we often watched
have left again,
their holes in the cliff-face
look down where sand falls,
clay slips,
and a notice states
that this is an unstable place.

For you, on this bright day,
winter almost here,
no place.

Spots and patches of light
dance as the waves break.
White light,
greeny-grey water,

ash that is blown back
and waves fetch and cover.

Now, for the first time,
you who would gladly comfort,
look away.

★

What is the scent on the salt air?
I search, and find
a few late flowers:
sweet alyssum,
tiny white faces
among rocks, sea defences
of Portland stone.

Shall I lend you my senses
to know once more the finds
that every day delighted you
and bound you to the world?

I do not find you in this ash
that vanishes among the foam –

ash that is less than anything
you lingered over,
                              walking
counting pebbles shells
bladder wrack dulse
kelp with a holdfast stone.

It is not words that hold you
any more than shingle keeps
the water that sluices it,
sifts, running down,
changing its shape.

It is not you who dissolve
as I come to the edge of the shore.

A POEM FOR MY FATHER

'The first region is colour.'
H.W. Fawkner

November: a no-month grey sky
brings out the colours:
earth-red of a flowerpot in the garden,
brown soil and decaying leaves
washed fresh by rain.
The birch-tree is a yellow light
burning outside the window.

Inside, I pick over dead things:
a brush with stiff bristles,
tubes in an old paintbox,
battered and stained,
all magic gone except the names:
yellow ochre, burnt umber, cobalt blue . . .

*

Alkali or acid?
         It is knowledge
that dies with the man who knew soils,
expert on phosphate and nitrate, on mulch.
I see him in his old raincoat
fixing a garden line,
or treading down earth round the roots
of a young apple tree,
or pruning with a knife
curved like the horn of the moon.

He liked to say he came south
in a green winter, Yorkshire
edging his voice in the soft country.

We would hear him singing in the ward
as we came up the stairs –
death-knell of a fine baritone,
the romantic, handsome man
who liked women, single in his love.

Over his bed the painting of a cornfield
he could no longer see,
splashes of bright red,
bluish-green elms, the fullness
of summer days we could feel and smell.

★

It was fear also that he taught,
white-faced, his hand
electric in my hand – a man
hugging the wall by the stone steps,
following the hedge round the field,
crouching at the simultaneous
lightning bolt and thunder crack,
crying out,
          'Who should we help'.

Fear, and a pride
that might have been humility –
a man with Constable's
'God's gift of seeing', who avoided public view,
making his home his gallery.
   'A perfectionist,' he said,
'that's what I was' – an artist
who destroyed more pictures than he left,
who found a place out of his time,
and set up his easel by river
and in field corner
      painting
            impossible
                  peace.

★

I have never seen a stranger thing
than his dead face,
false smile on an effigy,
an immaculate, dressed up corpse.

Outside, a downpour,
the streets of Christchurch
running with water,
the Avon racing full,
spray jetting from tyres,
leaves whirling or dancing
or plastered to the road.

I could think of nothing, only
a story he liked to tell – when
he was a young man working in Scotland,
one day, he did not go out in the boat
which was caught in a storm on the loch,
was not drowned with his two companions,
as his landlady thought,
who ran about the house crying,
'Wheer's my laddie, wheer's my bonnie laddie?'

★

Oak branches tufted with grass
mark the winter floods. On banks,
between leafless trees, yellow
of primroses, first daffodils.

In the stillness,
a woodpecker's hammer-notes vibrating.
From a wooden bridge, I scatter ash
which the current gathers,
bears down,
moving in snaking lines,
smudging dark water,
reflections of branches and sky.

I follow the way of the water with my mind
        flowing –
through wood and meadow,
under Boldre Bridge,
past the Shallows, where he painted
and I fished with my first bamboo,
the quick mirror-surface distorting us,
as here, it twists the trees.
        And for a time
all seems colourless,
until I look close and see again
the darkest dark that is depth
of colour – sky-and-water mix
of yellow and blue and brownish green,
the surface bark, or a nest of snakes
shedding their skins,
flicker-tongued adders of fire
dissolving in depth, the bodied
escaping appearances,
the bodiless the broken the whole
        flowing through.

*

It is the knowledge that dies,
stories one half-remembers
without the voice,
no particle of the living
reducible to an image or a word.

        In this region
there are no appearances,
no painted surfaces, only fire
that burns with the life in things.

To hold it
is like putting your fingers in a flame,
or trying to bring back an object
from a dream –
treading down firmly on the stairs of water,
rising slowly to the air.
And at the last something clutches
at your wrist and you wake scared,
hand tingling, your empty, open hand.

NOT LIKE ICARUS

for my brother David

Not like Icarus – your white legs,
your strong, man's legs,
out of the water, up in the air, waving.
And I looking on from the shore
as you stood on your hands on the sea-bed –
astonished, longing to follow.

How powerful you seemed,
how indestructible,
your crawl into the waves
a total mastery,
your disappearance
a certain prelude to return,
hands dripping with treasure.

But water was not the element you loved.

I remember the silhouettes
on your bedroom wall, the diagrams,
the balsa-wood models –
Lancaster, Heinkel, Hurricane –
all the exotic names and shapes,
as strange to me as flint axes
and mammoth bones, but to you
the romance of the real, freedom
you would learn to master.

I don't believe in your death,
you are too much part of the world
that held you, free of the air,
as I once saw you when I was a boy
and you were a young man, diving
for a handful of gravel and mud,
waving to us with your legs, surfacing.

But words were not the poetry you wanted.

I remember the excitement
with which you ran from the house
at the noise of low-flying jets,
the look of a boy on your man's face
at the far-off sound of a speck
that seemed to float in the blue.

Nothing could compare with the drone
of the engine, ground spreading out,
cloud streaming past and the sun above,
your surge into the wide, blue sky.
Then you would dip again, down
to the earth that kept you
for a time but did not hold you.

MARCH

Even when he was blind,
a ninety year old man
confined to his chair,
my father would long to see
just one more spring.

In his voice the words
return to me,
with green leaves,
first celandines.
But already it is too late:
there is more growing
under any hedge than we can see.

Listen, then:
on a tree top far off
across a meadow,
a blackbird sings, gathering
the whole movement in his song.

KEATS IN WINCHESTER

for Elizabeth Bewick

What should poetry make,
Keats,
of your absence?
                    Poetry
that finds every thing
every place interesting.

Here, it is your Autumn still,
though burnt stubble spreads
its blackened hedgehog skins
across the downs, and smoke
clings to walls where the house
you lodged in stood, where
you lived again Tom's death
and lived your own, while
the landlady's son scraped his violin.

When smoke clears,
when the yellow hazel leaf
closed like a tiny hand
dances on invisible silk,
there is a light within the light,
which, like a spring-tide,
floats the city off its sunken base,
and gives a grace of sail to hulks of stone.

You are no shade
in the the valley of bones.

You have left no relic
where you loitered
reading a love letter,
on the cathedral floor
    sinking down
    down
    to the dead waters
            dragging down.

You have braved the dream –
the white face on the altar steps,
the fallen Titan's agony and rage.
Now it is finished –
           a fragment,
open on the desk,
as lightly you step out
through the Close, turn down
College Street, and walk
to the water-meadows,
leaving the place a living soul.

WRITERS' WORKSHOP

for Gillian Clarke

1. Ty Newydd

We have come here to write, if we can,
to make shapes of our thoughts and feelings,
perhaps to see what we are part of.

One man remembers magical sensations,
a woman writes about her sister who has died.

Each of us moves restlessly through a maze,
glimpsing older and younger backs or faces,
most of them our own.

Each also senses another presence,
which haunts us in different forms:

the silence of a factory in which the machines
are shrouded in dusty sheets,
the reverberating hush
of a battleground after armistice,
or a man who stamped his image on the world,
and came back here to die.

2. By Afon Dwyfor

It is an illusion, of course,
but at last the 'Great Commoner'
seems to have become part of the elements –
at one with the boulder built into his memorial,
and Afon Dwyfor swirling between boulders,
and woods of oak and beech and sycamore,
and alders dipping their leaves in the water.

3. Lloyd George Museum, Llanystumdwy

In one photograph,
a dark-haired poet looks up,
proudly, perhaps defiantly, his arms
laid on the arms of the bardic chair.

He is honoured by principalities
and powers, and perhaps humoured,
for the Statesman
who stands beside him, playing his part,
wears a slight smile.

It amazes me to recognise the poet,
who is still young.
           I saw him in old age:
Gwenallt, the skull
showing in his face
which was like parchment
where feeling had etched
the history of his people.

The dead, brown leaves
of the laurel wreath are not his.
It was thrown into the carriage
in which the Statesman drove
through London, with the King, returning
in triumph from Versailles.

Surely there are materials here
for a poem about history:
fifty years of cartoons
and newspaper photographs –
manhandled suffragettes
with the clothes clawed off their backs,
munitions, wars, faces in the maze . . .

4. Criccieth: the boy on the beach

Below the house,
out of the dusty empire of the sun,
field paths lead us
to a smell of wild roses and brine,
peeling, upturned boats, crab-shells
and fleshy, salt-loving plants.

Here it is always another world.
Two crows, out of an old ballad,
pick over kelp at the water's edge,
hop back when a wave breaks.

He would have been amused, the boy
who played on this pebbly beach,
and perhaps the old man, too,
standing here again,
all his powers, titles, names
                    a memory.

Small again,
with everything still to make,
his companions would be once more the powers that shape rock,
and make and unmake cloud,
which drifts over on a day that he feels will last for ever,
darkening, brightening.

IN THE FOOTSTEPS OF NO-ONE

in memory of R. S. Thomas

After the closed door, silence.

After the death-fog, emptiness.

After the emptiness, images –

    a shape of words,
we could say,
no bigger than a man's hand,
a cloud, a flock of birds whitening
the March ploughland, blackening
mountains & moorlands & the coasts of Wales,
a mist rising off moist furrows
and the earthen crock of a skull
with its question-mark curl of spirit.

Who is this man
who proclaims himself no-one?
What is his boast?

Old salt, lashed to the father-tree.
Priest on his knees, daring to question
He Who Is Not At Home.
Listener with his ear to the shell
of the church that was Wales,
waiting for a worthy people.

Proud man, nobly infirm, stag
sniffing the air for a rival.
Austere old man, suddenly
skipping like a youth
to the pleasures of his lady.

As for myself, I most remember
a night when his voice refused us
everything but the poem,
which seemed to reach out,
and quavering on the air
came an owl's voice from Powys woods
seeming to answer.

So the images, the cloud,
we might say,
the flock descending
appear to settle, and rise,
as a mist,
leaving moist blades shining.

Afterwards silence
that is a different sound,
the mountains, the moorland, the sea
and the sea-watches
sharper, brighter,
and more the same than we ever knew.

Like a door, we might say,
which the man has opened,
and closed behind him,
leaving it as it always was,
but now too strangely different,
the land of a poet who dared to be human.

HARDY OF WESSEX

To Donald Davie

We go back to him,
thinking we can read his face,
like the land's –
Mr Hardy's, writer,
late of Max Gate, Dorchester.

What we want him to be, he is:
our elegist, whose heart lies
in the mould that shaped it –
from which we conjure him,
melancholy as a robin in winter
whistling on a tomb.

He is our shade, but
it is we who haunt him, walking
the dungy by-ways, shadowing
the cloud-dark Dorset heights.

Still he looks down at us,
on the road he too struggled up,
scattered with the shards of our armies,
lit by the glare of nuclear fires.
We look back, reading in his face
the stories we tell ourselves,
that are not true.

FOR A WOMAN WHO SAID SHE COULD FALL IN LOVE
WITH A BOAT

for Mieke on her fiftieth birthday

What I wish you is not a sieve
or a chugging tub
or a hulk half sunk in the mud
with ribs that clutch at the sky,
but a sound bottom,
good timbers throughout
and oceans ahead to plunge in.

Or a canoe, maybe, or a kayak,
for mountain lakes and rivers,
skin or bark rider of rapids
and a wise spirit to guide you –
sickle-gleam glimpsed between cedars,
new moon drifter on dark water
                    bringing peace.

Or a rowboat,
oars dripping,
crawling in creeks – where you anchor,
and lie back, head pillowed,
and dream, rocking, rocking,
watching the sailing sky.

Or else a thoroughbred yacht,
sail taut as a fin or billowing,
gull-white hull with lines
sleek as a great northern diver –
a yacht which never dives, but cuts through waves
over the crab's den and the lobster's lair,
over stones and mud where the weeds are,
under, down under, while it races over
and ocean is its pasture.

Better for you a boat like a dolphin,
a mythical craft,
part mammal and part bird.
Nose up, nose down, and the back curves
out of the water, awash and shining.
What are you then but the sea
and the sea's daughter,
waves riding waves
and spume in your hair?

Best of all though I wish you
one of your native boats.
Not a *tjalk* with a hold
full of vegetables and household stuff,
or the floating barn of a flat-bottomed *aak,*
smelling of grain and stone to mend roads.
No grandfather barge which you would care for
like a beloved elder, retired
from the work of the world.

Rather an antique sailing boat
with brass portholes and polished timbers,
stately and playful and worthy
of every weather,
canal-wise and ocean-knowing,
a boat with an engine that never fails,
and room below when you carry a fellow voyager,

and a red sail.

THOUGHTS ON A STAR-MAP

for Lee on his fiftieth birthday

Venus bright
in the dawn sky
of your birth-month.

Jupiter and Saturn
crossing the sky
from east to west.

Think of light
travelling for a million years,
more than a million,
the astronomers' unimaginable
numbers and times,
but light which the eye sees:

Andromeda,
sister galaxy,
faint as a smudge of dust.

Think of the names
we pin on the sky. Imagine them
falling back like acid rain,
and the bright object,
without number or name,
swimming in its own light.

★

Time to begin.

A block of wood
lies on the studio floor –
a windthrown trunk
that was feathered with leaves.

New light flashes
through gaps in the roof
where lately swallows flew in,
cutting the air.

Think of the birds
flying away. Imagine the sound
of a human kiss
waved into space.
What will it find?
Who will know what we are?

A NOTE ON THE 'GROUNDWORK' POEMS

A NOTE ON THE
'GROUNDWORK' POEMS

'Ground' is a concept that has fascinated me for many years. At the time of my earlier poems, *Soliloquies of a Chalk Giant* (1974) and *Solent Shore* (1978), for example, I identified it with actual ground: chalk and soil and shingle, the material elements of place, which I sought to explore as a total environment, a human and nonhuman world in time and space. It may be that in that period I had a simpler and more secure idea of belonging to a historical community, which I owed in part to living in Wales, and to the influence of Welsh poets, while grounding myself imaginatively on my original home country in the south of England.

My later work has grown out of my earlier writing, but with a difference. It has become more exploratory, less sure of where I personally 'belong', and of what the human ground (*humus*) actually consists of, and what it rests on, what its foundation in metaphysical reality is. I am still drawn powerfully to the materiality of ground, and to all the forces, human and nonhuman, that go to the shaping of place; but I am now more aware of groundlessness. This has its positive and negative aspects. It can manifest itself as a sense of emptiness, an underlying void, and an accompanying disintegration of self. It can also be felt as what Lee Grandjean calls 'that ground of elemental energy from which all matter emerges and into which all things are eventually enfolded'. In this latter respect, it is associated with possibility, with loss of ego boundaries in an enlarged sense of being, and with imaginative energy that both makes and breaks images, in an attempt to intimate the power beyond images, on which all life depends.

My collaborative work with Lee Grandjean began in the 1980s, and found expression in *Their Silence a Language* (Enitharmon Press, 1993). It has been important from the beginning that we do not illustrate each other's work; what connects us, rather, is an imaginative 'field', in which, each in the terms of his own art, we work out concerns that we hold in common.

The 'Groundwork' poems were initially written for a collaboration with Lee Grandjean, commissioned by the Djanogly Art Gallery, University of Nottingham Arts Centre, and a selection of them formed part of the 'Groundwork' exhibition held at the Gallery (21 August–20 September 1998). The main, but not exclusive setting of 'Workpoints' is Moor Farm and the area immediately around it, in Norfolk, where Lee Grandjean and his family live. The title means what it says: the poems introduce 'points' to work on. These include, in a millennial context, both the old pattern of life, visible in the landscape and its medieval churches and their symbols, and the new sense of uncertainty and possibility, manifest in scientific exploration of the universe and the thought of a theoretical physicist such as David Bohm. These poems, but more especially 'From Debris', are what I think of as 'object' poems, 'cut' from their materials in a way analogous to carving. 'City Walking (1)' was written following a walk in London with Grandjean as companion and guide.

Together with the 'object' poems, and 'Moor Farm 1996', 'Groundwork' consists of 'Seven Songs', which are characterized by their fluidity. The voice of these is conceived as being female, not in the form of a woman persona, but as a kind of androgynous imaginative space, in which I attempt to transcend the limitations of both male and female egos. My aim in adopting a voice that dissolves the identity of polarized gender is to explore grounds of possibility, including hopes for a new life, free of the burdens and destructiveness of the past, and a sense of the strangeness of human being. In Grandjean's sculpture and drawing I apprehend shapes of new relationship especially between humankind and nature. My own concern with this subject focuses particularly on the connection between male and female elements in the individual psyche, and on the hope that a marriage of different energies may activate a new conception of the creative possibilities of our human ground.

In 'Workpoints' the quotations 'The dull mind rises to truth through that which is material' and 'God is nearer to us than our own Soul: for He is Ground in whom our Soul standeth' are from Abbot Suger of St Denis and Julian of Norwich respectively. The words italicized in the part beginning 'I like the face of this/theoretical physicist' are quoted from David Bohm, *Wholeness and the Implicate Order.*